Gra

RITA RAY

Published by Scholastic Ltd,
Villiers House,
Clarendon Avenue,
Leamington Spa,
Warwickshire CV32 5PR

© **1997 Scholastic Ltd**
1 2 3 4 5 6 7 8 9 0 7 8 9 0 1 2 3 4 5 6

Author Rita Ray
Editor Irene Goodacre
Series designer Joy White
Designer Claire Belcher
Illustrations Garry Davies
Cover illustration Frances Lloyd
Cover photograph Martyn Chillmaid

Designed using Aldus Pagemaker
Printed in Great Britain by Ebenezer Baylis & Son, Worcester

British Library Cataloguing-in-Publication Data
A catalogue record for this book is
available from the British Library.

ISBN 0-590-53460-2

Acknowledgements
The publishers gratefully acknowledge permission to
reproduce the following copyright material:
Margaret Wiley for 'OK Gimme' by Martyn Wiley from
OK Gimme © 1985 Martyn Wiley (1985, Versewagon Press).
Ian McMillan for 'What's It?' from *My First Has Gone
Bonkers* edited by Brian Moses © 1993, Ian McMillan
(1993, Blackie Children's Books).

Contents

Introduction

The acquisition of language is our most fundamental and important achievement. Children use the rules of grammar before they understand them. They have acquired these rules steadily since babyhood, and come to school with much implicit knowledge of grammar. The teacher's role is to extend and foster this grammatical knowledge. Teaching the rules of grammar raises awareness of how language works and gives children some control over its use. In *Children's Writing and Reading: Analysing Classroom Language* (Blackwell, 1984), Katharine Perera writes, 'In order for such intervention to succeed it has to work in harmony with the natural sequence of language acquisition.'

The material in this book is designed to cater for children at various stages of language development and to address the range of grammatical knowledge outlined in the UK national curricula for primary English. It provides teachers with flexible, easy-to-use activities which support the teaching of grammar, using the kind of language and situations which are familiar to primary-age children.

The activities should be used in a flexible way, selected by the teacher to complement class work. The grammar skills and knowledge will be more easily retained by the children if they fit into a context than if they are presented in isolated exercises.

Traditionally, grammar is understood to mean the structure of sentences, clauses and phrases. These cannot be considered in isolation but should be seen in relation to how we bring meaning out of spoken words and written text. Children should be aware that grammar relates to how we *use* language in everyday situations, it is not a dry subject dealt with only in school.

The activities are written in accordance with the requirements of the UK national curricula for English. In general terms, there is a requirement that children should use the vocabulary and grammar of standard English, though it is stressed that standard English is not the same as 'received pronunciation' and can be expressed in a variety of accents. At Key Stage 1 of the National Curriculum for England and Wales, the programme of study states that children 'should be introduced with appropriate sensitivity to the importance of standard English.' This can be done through role-play and games in a way that will not undervalue the language, dialect or accent that the child brings from home. For 'what belongs to language is a whole culture' (Wittgenstein) and a child may perceive criticism of the way he or she speaks as a criticism of a whole way of life. There is emphasis on knowledge about language in all the national curricula, and differences can be made interesting and exciting if they are presented in a positive way.

The book is divided into five sections, each representing a 'topic' in grammar – the alphabet, structure, punctuation, language study and parts of speech. There is, inevitably, some overlap as language does not fall neatly into single categories. Within the topics there are activities at different levels. These can be used separately, to differentiate the activity, or in a progressive way.

About the author

Rita Ray teaches English to trainee teachers and writes poems and stories for children.

Alphabet

Letters of the alphabet are the smallest units of our language. Understanding alphabetical order, and familiarisation with letter frequency and letters which are likely to occur together, enhance children's understanding of the basic building blocks of language.

Decorated letters This is a basic 'fun' activity to familiarise children with capital letter shapes and to differentiate them from lower case letters.
Dictionary drop The device of the dropped dictionary offers children practice in putting words into alphabetical order. Children who complete the activity quickly could be challenged to create some of the missing alphabet pages.
Alphabetical order This activity provides alphabetical order tasks of increasing difficulty. The page could be stuck into the back of the child's book and used to periodically check knowledge of alphabetical order. The activity could be extended by challenging children to check the meanings of all the listed words.

Find the vowels The various activities on this sheet focus on vowels and the fact that most words need vowels.

The vowel vulture This activity focuses on the identification of vowels in a well known rhyme. The use of 'y' to replace vowels is also introduced. Children might be asked to find more words which use 'y' – perhaps some where the 'y' is situated somewhere other than at the end, such as myth, hymn or gypsy.

Friendly letters and **More friendly letters** These activities raise awareness of pairs of letters which often occur together. The first deals with commonly-used vowels, while the second introduces a range of familiar double consonant sounds. Children could be encouraged to look out for paired letters in their own writing.

Fun alphabets This activity reinforces alphabetical order by asking children to complete two 'themed' alphabets. Point out that a little 'cheating' is allowed on 'x'! Encourage the children to use reference books for assistance.

Structure

The activities in this section provide opportunities for pupils to explore the ways written and spoken language are organised to communicate meaning. They should stimulate both practical engagement with the building blocks of language (words, phrases, sentences) as well as reflective consideration on pupils' own use of language to structure speech and writing and to make sense of texts.

Signs of autumn This activity develops awareness of the subject and predicate structure in sentences, although the terms are not used. The given sentences provide a model for the children's own sentences.

What are they saying? Word order is one of the most characteristic features of English. Changing the order of the words can change the meaning of the sentence. Help the children to discover that the capital letters and punctuation marks can be used as clues to determine the first and last words in the sentences.

All mixed up The completed story derives its humour from wordplay, encouraging an interest in words and their use and interpretation in different contexts.

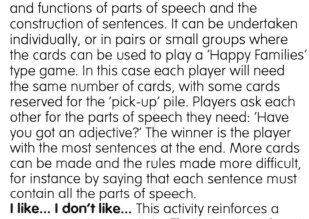

Pick and mix This activity focuses on the names and functions of parts of speech and the construction of sentences. It can be undertaken individually, or in pairs or small groups where the cards can be used to play a 'Happy Families' type game. In this case each player will need the same number of cards, with some cards reserved for the 'pick-up' pile. Players ask each other for the parts of speech they need: 'Have you got an adjective?' The winner is the player with the most sentences at the end. More cards can be made and the rules made more difficult, for instance by saying that each sentence must contain all the parts of speech.

I like... I don't like... This activity reinforces a common sentence pattern. The instructions do not specify the number of sentences to be written. This can be limited if necessary according to the ability of the child.

Dear diary The diary format provides a pattern for constructing sentences in the past tense. Draw children's attention to the verbs they have used and how the past tense has been formed – for example, by adding 'd' or 'ed'.

Pyramids This activity presents children with a visual image for building sentences. Discuss which words are most important for giving basic meaning to a sentence and how meaning is refined with the addition of words.

Senses poem This activity provides a pattern for the children's writing, but also allows them to think up creative images for their poems.

Picture code This activity structures sentence making by drawing attention to the various types of words in sentences. Children are challenged to 'decode' a sentence which combines function words with pictograms. This then provides the code that allows the children to construct their own sentences.

The glomps This activity uses nonsense words to focus attention on word endings and word position in a sentence, and to demonstrate the children's understanding of grammar. They will enjoy sharing their ideas about the meaning of 'glomp', 'roggling' and 'vangle'.

Nonsense poem This activity reinforces the children's ability to choose the right parts of speech to structure sentences.

Missing words This activity employs techniques of cloze and sequencing to extend the children's understanding of language structure.

Secret rhymes The omission of words from well-known rhymes develops children's ability to predict syntactic structure.

Talking to the aliens This activity helps children to think about the basic structure of language by inventing their own.

Tongue-twister and **Tongue-twister sentence** These activities provide further opportunities to construct sentences, this time with an aspect of alliteration. The first activity requires children to choose alliterative adjectives. The second activity, a bit more difficult, requires them to construct an alliterative sentence. The children can attach the tongues to the faces by using a solid gluestick. The 'tongues' can then be rolled up and secured with a small amount of Blu-Tack.

Why do you like it? The book review format provides a pattern for constructing sentences using the language of explanation, evaluation or persuasion.

Mixed-up story This sequencing activity develops children's ability to put events into a logical order, using indicators of time and other sequence clues. The ability to sequence is important in all areas of language and is frequently demanded in other curriculum subjects.

Draw the pictures, The Christmas fair and **The smugglers** These modelling activities indicate children's understanding of what they read by asking them to draw the pictures they describe. The three activities become progressively more difficult.

Thank-you notes This activity provides an opportunity to discuss the characteristic format and language of letter writing in the context of thank-you notes. Ask the children who might give them each of the unappealing and inappropriate presents. Support is offered by a word bank of key vocabulary.

My point of view This activity requires the children to write in the first person from the point of view of an inanimate object. It is, therefore, an ideal opportunity to discuss the features of first-person writing. The letter format in which they are asked to write gives further practice in this genre.

Animal agony aunt This activity develops the use of persuasive, exhortatory language in a humorous context.

Pen-friend from outer space An alien pen-friend provides an audience for descriptive writing about well-known topics, giving children the opportunity to demonstrate their use of adjectives and adverbs and their ability to link sentences coherently.

Who are they? This activity gives opportunities to compose sequenced sentences in response to a picture stimulus. Look for and emphasise the importance of descriptive language.

Run to the wall This cloze activity provides a model for instructional text and develops the ability to predict which parts of speech will complete simple sentences.

How to make a dinosaur This activity gives practice in sequencing instructions, then tests understanding through the modelling task of drawing what has been described.

Hide-and-seek The children are asked to reflect on a well-known game and to derive the rules. This gives them a context in which to use logic and to express themselves clearly and succinctly. Discuss the features of instructional writing – short, concise sentences that are obviously sequenced (often numbered) and use temporal words such as now, then, before, after, first, finally.

Spiral adventure This open-ended activity is designed to allow the children to create their own rules for a board-game. This gives them opportunities to demonstrate their knowledge of the features of rule-writing.

Invent a game The main objective of this activity is to offer children opportunities to make up rules and to communicate them clearly. They should be encouraged to modify their rules once they have tried them out.

Stick to the rules! This rule-writing activity requires children to make rules for members of their family, pets and friends. While this demands the logical, imperative structure of rules it also allows them to use more personal and subjective language.

Family trees and **Word endings** Word endings change the meaning and function of words. Raising children's awareness of word families and root words will increase their knowledge of language. These two activities demonstrate how words with new meanings may be formed when common suffixes are added to root words.

Tall tales The task of writing an unlikely tale, using a poem as a starting point, is designed to extend imagination and vocabulary.

Silly similes This activity introduces the structure and concept of similes using 'as'. This is done in the form of: (noun) as (adjective) as (noun) – 'gorillas as noisy as raspberries'. Children enjoy the absurdity of this game and it's fun to read out the similes in mock poetic style. The nouns can be kept in one or two piles – whichever works better for the child or group.

Agreeable verbs Children should be introduced to the concept of subject-verb agreement even if the grammatical terms are not used. They will readily recognise inconsistencies in speech, so oral work should be the starting point for this type of activity.

Direct and indirect Following examples, this activity encourages the children to identify direct and indirect speech, and gives models to support the task of putting a piece of dialogue into indirect speech. The activity can be used to teach or review the punctuation of direct speech.

What's the big idea? and **Put them together** These activities introduce the concept of main and subordinate clauses. This type of grammatical analysis gives useful practice in developing children's understanding of the grammar of complex sentences.

Tall, taller, tallest; Messy, messier, messiest and **Good, better, best** To facilitate the development of knowledge and skills in this area of grammar the three activities for comparison of adjectives are differentiated into three different levels – the first deals with regular versions, the second covers those which change spelling, and the third moves on to irregular examples.

Bigger and better poems This activity gives opportunities to develop and demonstrate knowledge of comparison of adjectives.

You're the most Children can practise use of superlatives as they create their own poem.

Punctuation

Punctuation gives clues to grammatical structure. It marks beginnings and endings of sentences and indicates questions, as well as guiding intonation and expression. Punctuation marks are not just an addition to writing but an integral part of it.

After children have developed the ability to structure sentences, the next step is to confirm the structure by marking it with punctuation. Children tend to overuse punctuation at first, but this is a normal stage in the learning process and improves with practice.

Children need to recognise and use punctuation marks on a regular basis, so some of the activities focus on receptive skills, requiring children to notice and take account of the marks; while in other activities practice is given in the actual use of punctuation marks.

Name it This activity focuses on the use of capital letters for proper names.

Jellysock The use of capital letters and full stops is practised, giving opportunities to show understanding of basic sentence structure.

Take a break! A model is given for the use of the comma in punctuating lists. Children are then challenged to add commas to another list, and finally to create and punctuate their own list.

Time to pause This activity gives the children practice in using the comma to punctuate continuous prose.

What's the question? This basic activity introduces question marks. Practice is given in writing question marks and in their use.

Riddle muddle The children show understanding of question and answer format by matching the right answers to riddles and adding question marks where appropriate.

Guess the questions This activity develops the use of the question and answer format in the context of an interview in which the children are provided with answers, then asked to make up the questions.

Asking questions This activity further develops the ability to formulate questions as well as that of turning simple statements into questions.

Halt! Danger! Help! and **Shock horror game!** The use of exclamation marks is introduced, first focusing on their recognition in context, progressing to practice in using exclamation marks appropriately.

The word-shortening machine The device of a function machine, which the children may have met in a different context, is used to introduce contracted forms, such as 'don't', and to give practice in writing these forms.

Whose pet?, Spot the apostrophes and **Gina's gerbil** These progressive activities develop the children's ability to recognise and use the possessive apostrophe.

Who's talking? The use of speech marks is modelled and practice in writing out conversations is given.

Language study

The range of spoken and written English within children's own experience is the starting point for developing an awareness of the fascinating variety and complexity of language in general. Word origins and meanings, the appropriateness of different registers for different audiences, codes and messages, fact and fiction genres – these are all areas covered within the activities in this section aimed at heightening children's knowledge about, and interest in, language.

Reasons to write A format is given for the children to note the kinds of writing they do or encounter during the course of a day. The activity focuses attention on the varied purposes of, and audiences for, writing.

Secret messages Through picture messages the concept of the evolution of writing systems is introduced, focusing on the basic principles of communication.

Word origins This activity looks at word origins, a fundamental and fruitful area of language study. Encourage the children to use an etymological dictionary, and point out that they may come up with different information.

Foreign exchange This activity draws attention to words we have imported into English from other languages and investigates their origins and meanings. The children will need access to dictionaries, and may find differing origins or meanings to the words they are investigating.

Top ten words The top ten most used words are introduced in this activity, raising children's awareness of high frequency words in the English language.

Treasure chest and **Nice words** An important step in the extension of writing skills is learning to use a thesaurus. This skill is introduced in these activities where children need to be shown how to use a thesaurus to find alternatives to words in the given passages.

Favourite stories Discuss with the children the different types of fiction genre. Encourage them to identify features of their favourite stories in order to build up knowledge about the characteristics of the different genre types.

Fact and fiction Examples of fact and fiction are given so that children can identify the differences and develop an understanding of their features. If possible visit the school library to collect examples of fact and fiction books on the same subject. Give the children time to look through these.

Finding your way around books This activity requires children to undertake specific tasks to show their understanding of the differences between fiction and non-fiction texts. Challenge the children to draw some conclusions about the characteristics of fiction and non-fiction texts from their completed tick chart. For example: *Fiction books do not usually have an index.*

Modern fairy tale Discuss the features of traditional fairy tales and ask children if they know of any 'modern' fairy tales – for example *The Three Little Wolves and the Big Bad Pig* by Helen Oxenbury (Heinemann). The activity supports the children's writing by giving some starter sentences and some modern words.

What does it mean? This activity develops the ability to differentiate between informal 'playground' language and standard English.

Language map The 'language map' is a useful device for focusing children's attention on the language they hear spoken in order to compare language in different contexts. A developed 'ear' for spoken language is a valuable asset for writers of any age.

Poems to say aloud Allow children to collect spoken words and phrases over a period of time and record them in the space provided. Then encourage them to choose those with a common theme to form the basis of their poem, as in the given example.

Banana split The task of writing a recipe from an oral account focuses on the difference between spoken and written language. Children are asked to take the facts from a conversation and turn them into a set of instructions.

What would you like? Children are asked to write out what two characters will say when ordering items from a menu. This gives further practice in acknowledging the differences between spoken and written English.

Opposites This activity introduces antonyms. Children are first asked to match antonyms, then come up with some independent examples.

Sounds like... Homophones are words that sound the same but have different meanings and usually different spellings (for example: plane, plain). This activity will draw children's attention to the fact that there are alternative ways of spelling the same sound.

Different words – same meaning This activity introduces synonyms and offers the children practice in recognising and using them.

Same and different The children's knowledge of synonyms and antonyms can be demonstrated as they work through the various activities on this sheet.

Place-names and **Name that place!** These two activities provide opportunities to explore the history of language by considering, then finding, the original meanings of place-names.

Monster bargains and **Astronaut specials** These activities give the children insight into the use of persuasive language, as used in advertising. Raising awareness of this use of language prepares and enables children to be critical about material presented to them in a variety of media.

The puppet show This activity requires the children to choose language to communicate essential information in a poster format. They should also try to make the poster attractive and easy to read.

The amazing snowball machine This activity requires children to use language descriptively and persuasively.

Notes and letters: 1 and **2** These two sheets provide models and opportunities for children to write for different purposes and audiences, and therefore in different 'registers'. Discuss with them how written standard English varies in degrees of formality.

Which way? In this activity children are encouraged to consider the clear and concise language required when giving directions. Ensure, in advance, that the children know left from right.

Telling the story The task of describing an accident to different audiences gives practice in using registers appropriate to a variety of people and situations.

Police report This activity follows on from the previous one, as the children are asked to finish a police witness account of the accident described on page 112. This will give them an opportunity to practise writing appropriately for a formal report.

Parts of speech

Learning the parts of speech not only gives children an understanding of how sentences are constructed, but also provides them with the vocabulary needed to talk about it. They will then go on to have more control over the composition of their own writing and, when reading, a greater appreciation of how text fits together.

Name the object This activity can be used to introduce or to reinforce the term and concept of 'noun'.

Test your memory Use this memory game to reinforce the idea that nouns are the names of objects. When the children have written their story, ask them to identify all the words in it that are nouns.

Describing places, Describing things, Describing a person and **Describing a character** These activities provide models for the children to follow as they draw pictures, then use a thesaurus to find suitable adjectives to describe their pictures.

Diamond poems and **Same sound list poems** Poem formats are used here as a device to encourage children to choose and combine suitable nouns and adjectives. The second activity also focuses on alliteration.

Word inventions In this activity a set of cards containing nouns is provided. The cards can be cut up and put together in both conventional and novel ways to make new words. Discuss with the children how, when this is done, the first noun in the new word serves the same function as an adjective – it describes the second noun.

What are they doing? This activity asks the children to identify verbs. Support is offered in the form of pictures.

Message in a bottle In this activity the function of verbs is demonstrated in the context of a short message. The children go on to identify verbs in their own writing.

In the future Examples of the use of the future tense are given as models for children to write their own passage in the future tense. Ask them to identify the three ways in which the future tense is indicated – *shall*, *will* and *going to*.

What did you do? A spoken example of the use of the past tense is given as a model to encourage children to write their own passage in the past tense.

Yesterday, today and tomorrow This activity gives children the opportunity to demonstrate their understanding of both regular and irregular verbs in the past, present and future tenses. Children could be encouraged to write a diary, underlining the past tense verbs.

Time machine in the future and **Time machine in the past** In these activities the time machine device permits more extensive use of both past and future tense in pieces of creative writing.

How is it done?, **Underlining adverbs** and **Adverbs from adjectives** These activities explain the use of adverbs. On page 132 children are given examples of how certain adverbs are formed from adjectives.

Word quilt This activity provides practice in distinguishing nouns, verbs, adjectives and adverbs. It can be adapted to use a different set of words, and it would be possible to focus on one particular part of speech.

Where is it?, **Read and draw**, **Where does it go?** and **Put it where?** In these activities the use of prepositions is demonstrated and children are required to show their understanding by reading, writing and drawing.

The untidy room game: 1 and **2** The purpose of this game is to show understanding of prepositions by drawing objects in the right place on the sheet after questioning a partner. Two children should play the game together – one will need sheet 1 and the other sheet 2. They should not show each other the sheets.

Who did what? The purpose of this activity is to give practice in the use of pronouns. Children are challenged to choose the correct pronoun to replace given nouns.

He, she, it and **Fill the gaps** These progressive activities require the children to first identify pronouns, then replace given nouns with pronouns and, finally, to supply pronouns to fill gaps in sentences.

What's 'it'? In this activity the children are encouraged to write riddles using pronouns, the model being a poem called *What's 'it'?* by Ian Macmillan, which is like a riddle, replacing its subject with 'it'. (The answer to the riddle is 'time').

Make a connection This activity gives practice in the use of the conjunctions 'and', 'but' and 'because'. In the early stages of writing children often over-use 'and', but having mastered simple punctuation are ready to learn the appropriate use of conjunctions to connect words, clauses or sentences.

Skills index

Skill	Activity page number
Adjectives	26, 58, 63–67, 116–121, 132–133
Adverbs	26, 130–133
Advertising	105–108
Alliteration	37–38, 121
Alphabet- alphabetical order	15–22
	16–17, 22
Antonyms	99, 102
Apostrophes	79–81
Articles	26
Audience	109–110, 112
Capital letters	15, 68–69
Clauses	61–62
Commas	70–71
Comparison	63–67
Comprehension	41–43
Concept of language	36, 83, 87
Conjunctions	144
Contractions	78
Descriptive language	47–48, 116–119
Diary	28
Dictionary	16, 85–86
Directions	111
Evaluative language	39
Exclamation marks	76–77
Fact and fiction	90–93
Figurative language	58
First person	45
Full stops	69
History of language	85–86
Homophones	100
Instructions	49–50
Letter patterns	20–21
Letter writing	44–47, 109–110
Messages	31, 84, 124
Notes	109–110
Nouns-	26, 58, 114–115, 120–122, 133
proper	68, 103–104

Skill	Activity page number
Opposites	99, 102
Oral language	94–98, 112
Parts of speech	26, 32–35, 114–144
Persuasive language	46, 105–108
Place names	103–104
Poetry	30, 33, 57, 96, 120–121, 141, 143
Point of view	45
Prepositions	134–139
Pronouns	140–143
Punctuation	68–82
Question marks	72–75
Recipe	97
Registers	109–113
Report writing	113
Riddles	73, 143
Rules	51–54
Sentence structure	23–35, 61–62, 133
Sequencing	40, 50
Similes	58
Speech–	
direct/indirect	24, 60, 94–98
marks	82
Standard English	94–98
Subject/predicate	23
Subject/verb agreement	59
Suffixes	55–56
Synonyms	88–89, 101–102
Thesaurus	88–89, 101–102
Tongue-twisters	37–38
Verbs	26, 123–129, 133
tenses	28, 125–129
Vocabulary	57, 93
Vowels	18–19
Word–	
families	55–56
order	24–26
origins	85–86, 103–104

14

Decorated letters

✤ Fill each letter with capitals, then decorate the letters.

Example:

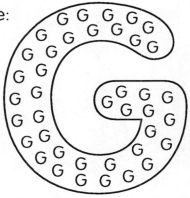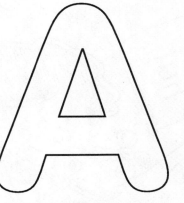

✤ Now draw and decorate some more capital letters.

Alphabetical order

Name _____

Dictionary drop

Shahnaz has dropped her word book.   ♣ Can you put these pages back in the right order?

1. ____Hh____   2. _____   3. _____   4. _____   5. _____   6. _____

Alphabetical order

♣ Put these lists into alphabetical order.

1	Look at the first letters.		

	zoo	1	_____
	when	2	_____
	mark	3	_____
	ghost	4	_____
	condense	5	_____
	abstract	6	_____
	under	7	_____
	star	8	_____
	egg	9	_____
	part	10	_____

3 This time look at the first, second and third letters.

	quite	1	_____
	cabbage	2	_____
	yell	3	_____
	hot	4	_____
	orange	5	_____
	yet	6	_____
	quack	7	_____
	house	8	_____
	card	9	_____
	ordinary	10	_____

2 Remember to look at the first and second letters!

	noose	1	_____
	bread	2	_____
	frog	3	_____
	valley	4	_____
	tree	5	_____
	victim	6	_____
	nettle	7	_____
	blend	8	_____
	fish	9	_____
	this	10	_____

4 The final challenge!

	install	1	_____
	instruction	2	_____
	instance	3	_____
	instant	4	_____
	instinct	5	_____
	instep	6	_____
	instalment	7	_____
	instead	8	_____
	instrument	9	_____
	institution	10	_____

Find the vowels

Once upon a time there were three bears.
They lived in a cottage in the wood.

a b c d **e** f g h **i** j k l m n **o** p q r s t **u** v w x y z

a e i o and u are the **vowels**.

Words need vowels.

❧ Read the sentences in the flag.

❧ Colour the vowels yellow.

How many times did you colour 'e'?

❧ Colour the vowels on the three bears' cottage.

The vowel vulture

The vowel vulture has eaten all the vowels in the rhyme below.

♣ Can you put them back?

J__ck __nd J__ll w__nt __p the h__ll

T__ f__tch __ p__ __l __f w__t__r.

J__ck f__ll d__wn __nd br__k__ h__s cr__wn

__nd J__ll c__m__ t__mbl__ng __ft__r.

Sometimes words use a 'y' instead of a vowel, as in the words sk**y** and fl**y**.

♣ Put in 'y' to read these words.

tr__   dr__   butterfl__

♣ Finish the 'y' pattern on this butterfly.

Friendly letters

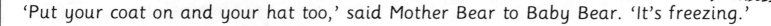

Some letters like to stay together.

♣ Look for these pairs in the story.
    oo ee oa ai ea

♣ Underline any you find.

The three bears went into the wood.

'Put your coat on and your hat too,' said Mother Bear to Baby Bear. 'It's freezing.'

Baby Bear looked for his green balloon while Father Bear put his boots on.

♣ Draw the pictures.

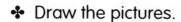

Three green trees.   A red coat.   Father Bear's boots.

More friendly letters

These letters often go together.

ch sh th st ing qu le

❧ Say the sounds they make.

❧ Look for these letter pairs
in the list of words opposite.

❧ Circle any that you find.

them

mosque

church

shop

stand

running

temple

ch	sh	th	st	ing	qu	le

❧ Find some more words which use these letter pairs and write them in the boxes.

Fun alphabets

♣ Finish the alphabet of food.

Apple pie
Banana split
Carrot cake
Damson jam
E
F
G
Hot dog
I
J
K
L
M
N
O
P
Q
R
S
Toffee
U
V
W
mixed biscuits
Y
Z

♣ Can you find animal names to finish this alphabet?

A
B
C
D
Elk
Fox
G
H
I
J
K
L
M
N
O
P
Quail
R
S
T
U
Vole
W
axolotl
Yak
Z

♣ Make up some more fun alphabets.

Signs of autumn

✤ Finish these sentences.

✤ Draw a line from each beginning to the right ending.

The weather   turn brown.

The birds   fly away.

The leaves   goes down.

The days   gets colder.

The nights   get shorter.

The temperature   get longer.

✤ Now make up two sentences of your own about the signs of autumn.

Sentence word order

What are they saying?

♣ Put the words in the right order then write the sentences into the bubbles.

what Grandma eyes Oh you big have!

me together Put again. back

me house. Take Cinderella's to

axe! get Quick an me

frog. kiss want I don't to a

any you Have wool?

All mixed up

The words in these sentences are all mixed up.

♣ Write the sentences out again with the words in the right order. Then read the funny story that they tell.

Smith is Mr greengrocer. a

_____

six is He tall. feet

_____

has hair. He brown

_____

coat. wears green He a

_____

does weigh? he What

_____

weighs He potatoes.

_____

Constructing sentences

Pick and mix

✤ Cut out the cards.

✤ Use them to make different sentences.

Some of your sentences will sound funny!

The	tasty	sausage	sizzled	scrumptiously
article (art)	*adjective* (adj)	*noun* (n)	*verb* (v)	*adverb* (adv)

(art) The	(art) A	(art) A	(adj) tiny	(n) dog	(v) barked	(v) crashed	(adv) quickly
(art) The	(art) The	(art) A	(adj) wobbly	(n) mouse	(v) sizzled	(v) sailed	(adv) slowly
	(adj) fluffy	(adj) striped	(n) tiger	(n) sausage	(v) jumped	(adv) loudly	(adv) scrumptiously
	(adj) tasty	(adj) big	(n) ship	(n) skateboard	(v) squeaked	(adv) softly	(adv) happily

✤ Play a game like 'Happy Families' with a friend.

✤ Ask each other for the cards you need to make your sentences.

I like... I don't like...

❖ Make more sentences by adding to the lists.

I like people who:	I don't like people who:	I like food that:	I don't like food that:
are kind.	are bad-tempered.	is sweet and crunchy.	is wet and lumpy.

Name _____

Sentence patterns, using past tense

Dear diary

❖ Draw and write what you did last week.

On Sunday I

On Monday I

On Thursday I

On Friday I

On Tuesday I

On Wednesday I

On Saturday I

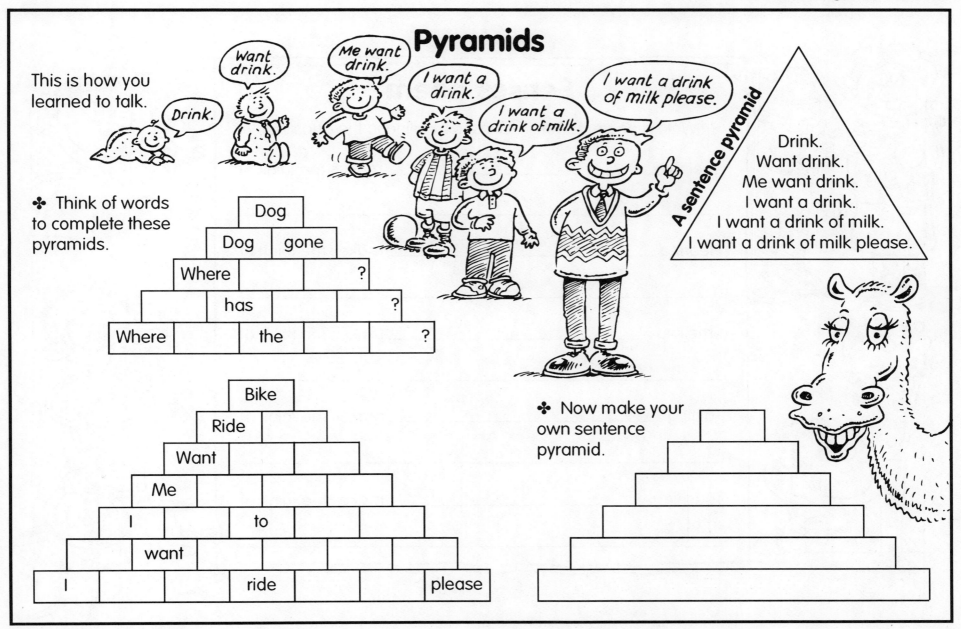

Pyramids

This is how you learned to talk.

Drink.

Want drink.

Me want drink.

I want a drink.

I want a drink of milk.

I want a drink of milk please.

A sentence pyramid

Drink.
Want drink.
Me want drink.
I want a drink.
I want a drink of milk.
I want a drink of milk please.

♣ Think of words to complete these pyramids.

	Dog		
Dog		gone	
Where			?
	has		?
Where		the		?

	Bike		
	Ride		
	Want		
	Me		
	I		to	
	want			
	I		ride		please

♣ Now make your own sentence pyramid.

Sentence patterns

Name _____

Senses poem

✤ Write a poem about the senses by filling in the gaps below.

Seeing _____ makes me think of

_____

Hearing _____ makes me think of

_____

Smelling _____ makes me think of

_____

Tasting _____ makes me think of

_____

Touching _____ makes me think of

_____

Picture code

✣ Look at this message.

The   boy   and   the   girl   sit   under   the   tree.

✣ Now read this one.

Was it easy?   ✣ Try this one.

Clues:

◉◎	◆	—	=	𐀪𐀪	🐱🐕
look	at	is	are	they	they
				(people)	(animals)

✣ Make up your own messages using the code.

The function of words in a sentence

Name _____

The glomps

❖ Read this sentence.

The glomps were roggling in the vangle.

❖ Answer these questions:

What were the glomps doing? _____

Where were they doing it? _____

❖ In the space provided draw a picture of the glomps roggling in the vangle.

❖ Compare your drawing of the glomps with your friends' pictures.

Nonsense poem

❖ Flick a counter, or roll a penny, and see which letter it lands on.

❖ Write a word beginning with that letter to continue the poem.

❖ Keep doing this until the poem is finished.

a	b	c	d	e	f
g	h	i	j	k	l
m	n	o	p	q	r
s	t	u	v	w	x
		y	z		

The first line has been written for you.   The counter landed on y, w, p and x

yams   wander   pulling   xylophones

_____

_____

_____

_____

❖ Now read out your nonsense poem.

The function of words in a sentence

Name _____

Missing words

♣ Put the words in the right spaces.

  Cinderella

Once upon a time _____ was a girl named

_____. She wanted to go _____ the ball,

but she _____ no dress and no _____.

'I want to go _____ the ball,' said Cinderella.

'_____ can't go,' said her _____.

'You have to clean _____ house.'

♣ Draw some pictures to show what happens in the story.

Secret rhymes

Be a word magician.

♣ Can you guess this well-known rhyme from just **one word**?!

_____ _____ ___ __ _ wall

_____ _____ ___ _ _____ ____

Did you guess? Here's the rest of the rhyme.

___ ___ _____ _____ ,

And ___ ___ _____ ___

_____' put _____ _____ again.

♣ Use the back of this page to write out some more well-known rhymes like this.

♣ Try them out on your friends.

Name _____

Talking to the aliens

Do you think aliens have a language?

☐ Yes ☐ No

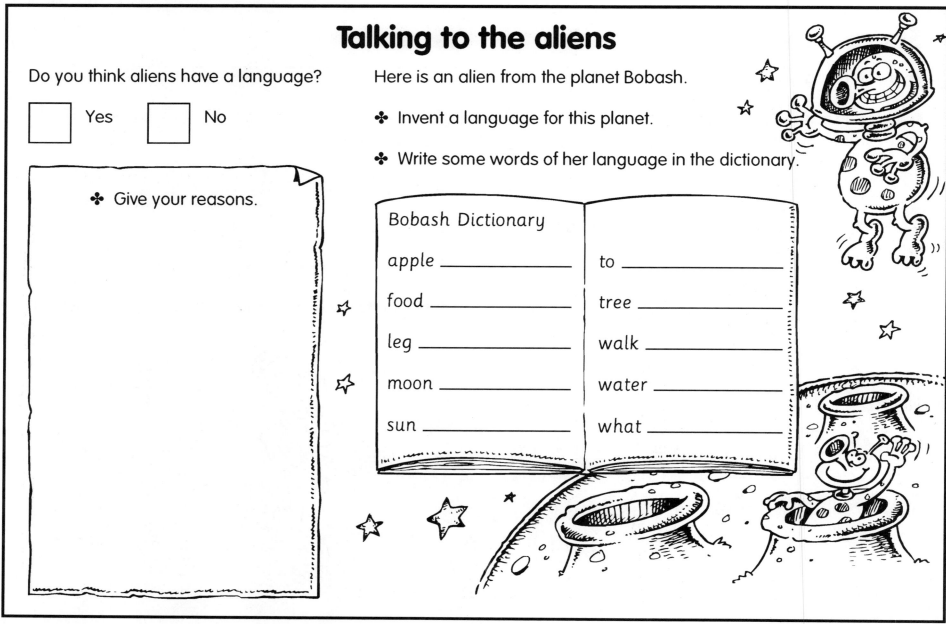

✤ Give your reasons.

Here is an alien from the planet Bobash.

✤ Invent a language for this planet.

✤ Write some words of her language in the dictionary.

Bobash Dictionary

apple _____ to _____

food _____ tree _____

leg _____ walk _____

moon _____ water _____

sun _____ what _____

Tongue-twister

a b c d e f g h i j k l m n o p q r s t u v w x y z

Imran has made up a tongue-twister.

slick
slippery
snappy
Sammy
snake

He chose a letter 's'
He found some words.
He tried them out.

slick   slippery

shape

snappy

snake   snoopy

✤ Choose a letter and write a tongue-twister of your own on a strip of paper.

✤ Draw a picture of a face and stick your tongue-twister on to it.

Making use of alliterative sentences

Tongue-twister sentence

Anna has made up a tongue-twister, but she wants to make it longer.

❖ Make up your own tongue-twister sentence.

❖ Then draw a picture of a face and stick on your tongue-twister.

Why do you like it?

❖ Choose a favourite story.

❖ Try to explain to others what the book is like.

Name of book: _____

Author: _____

Main characters: _____

_____

❖ Why do you like it? Continue writing on the back of this sheet if you need more space.

What is the story about?

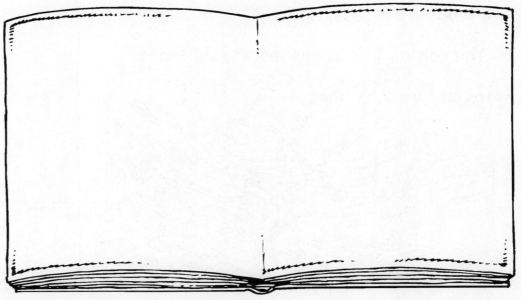

Name _____

Sequencing sentences

Mixed-up story

✤ Put the parts of the story in the right order. Then draw a picture about it.

1 __D__ 2 ____ 3 ____ 4 ____ 5 ____ 6 ____

A One day he jumped up in the air and landed by a pond two miles away.

B 'Where will we live now?' said the other frogs.

C When he jumped in the pond all the water flew out.

D Once upon a time there was a frog called Frank.

E 'You can all live in my shoes' said Frank.

F He had very big feet.

Draw the pictures

❖ Read these then draw a picture for each one.

Two cats sat on a rug. One cat was black with white paws. The other cat had black and grey stripes.	Tom sat at the table to eat his dinner. On his plate he had some chips, a piece of pizza and some beans.

Name _____

The Christmas fair

❖ Read the story, then draw the picture.

Mandy and Peter wanted to make things for the Christmas fair. They put four boxes on the table. There were two boxes full of wool. The wool was pink, yellow and blue. There was a box with bits of wood – long bits and short bits. The last box had a hammer, some nails and four knitting needles in it.

Name _____

The smugglers

♣ Read and draw.

It was midnight. Lisa and Mike were hiding behind a rock on the stony beach. Mike was holding a torch. It was switched off. A rowing boat was near the edge of the sea. Two men were carrying a big box between them. They had lifted it from the boat and were taking it towards a cave.

♣ What do you think was in the box?

_____

Letter writing

Name _____

Thank-you notes

❖ Write 'thank-you' notes for each of these rather unusual presents.

Here are some words and phrases you could use. Think of others if you can.

Dear	for	the	It is	It will be
very useful	beautiful		brilliant	
just what I wanted		Thank you		
Best wishes	Love			

My point of view

❖ Read this letter written by a swimming bag.

❖ Now write notes from your shoes and your lunch-box.

Dear _____

I am tired of having wet things dripping inside me. Last week your shampoo leaked. I can still smell it. You left me under your bed for a week. I got told off and thrown down the stairs.

From
Your swimming bag

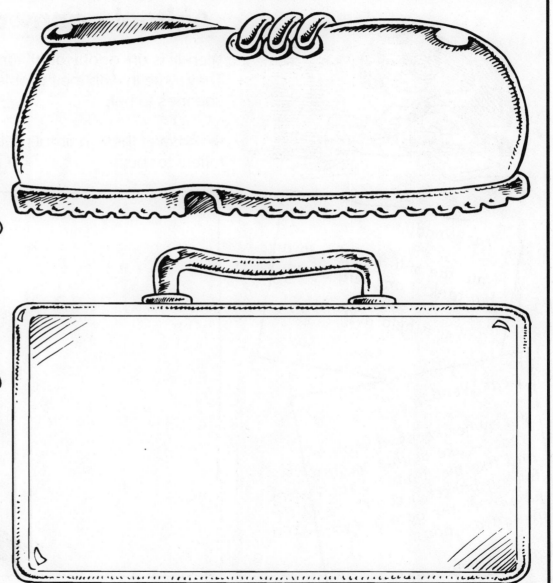

Name _____

Letter writing – persuasive language

Animal agony aunt

Wendy is an 'agony aunt' for animals. They write in with their problems and she tries to help.

✤ Answer these animal problem letters for her.

Dear Wendy,

I am the only goldfish in a big tank. I am very bored.

Can you help me?

Dear Wendy,

My owner keeps giving me treats – like double cream and fish pie. I am too fat for my basket. I can't jump over the gate or run away from dogs.

Can you help me?

Pen-friend from outer space

Your pen-friend from outer space has sent this picture to show you her home and family.

My name is Toozoo. I live on planet Voom. My planet has three suns. Here is a picture of my family and our pet. Do you like our house? Please tell me about your planet.

✤ Write to your pen-friend about where you live and your family.

Composing a passage from a picture stimulus

Who are they?

Who do you think these people are?   What are they thinking?   ✤ Write a few lines about each of them.

Run to the wall

♣ Read this to find out how to play the game.

♣ Finish the instructions.

1 Run to the _____.

2 _____ to five.

3 Turn _____.

4 Guess who _____ the _____.

5 If you are _____ you have to be on again.

6 If you are right, the person who has the _____ has to be on.

Sequencing instructions

How to make a dinosaur

✤ Put these instructions in the right order so that they tell you how to make a dinosaur.

A Paint a face on the small box.
B First, find some boxes.
C Last of all, stick a tail on your dinosaur.
D Paint the boxes.
E Pick a big, painted box for the body.
F Stick a small box on the body for a head.

1 __B__   2 ____   3 ____   4 ____   5 ____   6 ____

✤ Draw your model dinosaur.

Hide-and-seek

✤ Write the rules for playing hide-and-seek.

Name _____

Making up game rules

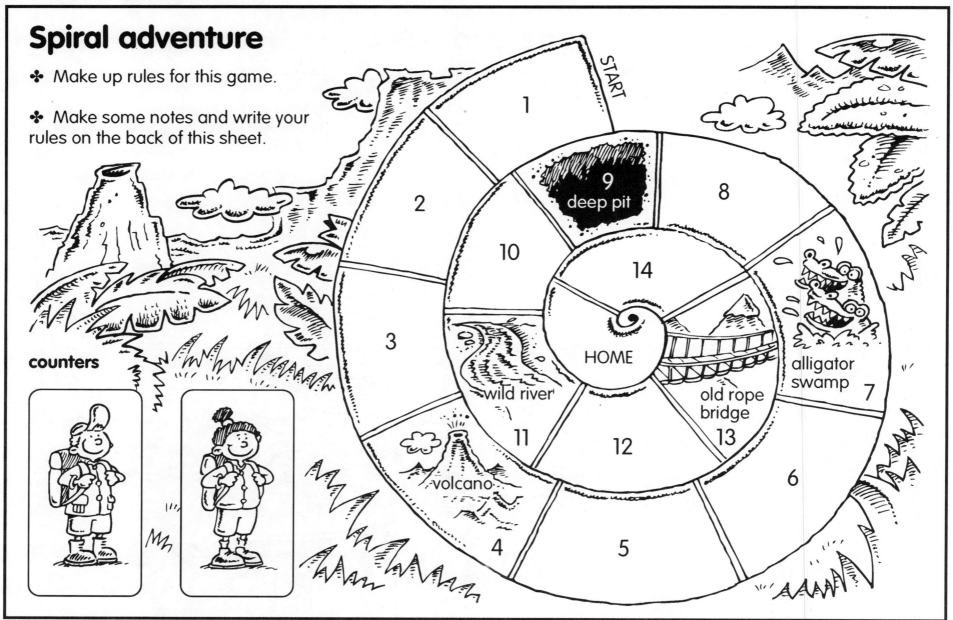

Spiral adventure

❧ Make up rules for this game.

❧ Make some notes and write your rules on the back of this sheet.

counters

Invent a game

♣ Invent a game of your own.

♣ Draw a picture of your game.

♣ Write the rules for it.

The name of my game is

_____

A picture of my game

The rules of my game _____

_____

_____

_____

_____

_____

_____

Writing rules

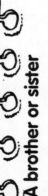

Stick to the rules!

✤ Write some rules for
● a brother or sister
● a pet dog
● a friend
● someone you know

A pet dog

1 Don't lick my face.

1

A brother or sister

1 Don't wake me up early.

A friend

1 Don't tell anyone my secrets.

Name _____

Family trees

♣ Try these endings on the words below. Some will fit and some will not.

| -ward | -less | -ness | -ish | -ly | -ing | -ed | -ful |

kind	slow	worth	life	home

♣ Now use the endings to 'grow' word families. The first one has been done for you.

Suffixes

Name _____

Word endings

-able   -ible

❧ Join the pieces to make four words.

 poss

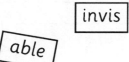 ible

able

 invis

suit

able

comfort

ible

❧ Make a list of other words ending in -ible or -able.

_____

_____

_____

_____

_____

_____

❧ Finish the table.
-ful   -less   -ness

rest	restful	restless	restlessness
use			
fear			
care			
hope			

Tall tales

Here is part of a poem called *Tall Tales*.

I know this old woman
who knows this old woman
who knows Red Riding Hood's grandma.

Well...I know this man
who knows this man
who can sing *Jingle Bells*
standing on his head
in a bucket of frogspawn.

We-e-ll...I know this girl
who knows this girl
whose great uncle
stood inside an erupting volcano
and got blown to China –
where he just sat down
and ordered chicken chow mein
with noodles.

No-o-o I don't believe it –
not noodles!

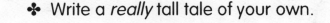

❖ Write a *really* tall tale of your own.

Similes

Name _____

Silly similes

✤ Cut out the noun and adjective cards.

✤ Put them face down in three piles.

✤ Pick up a card from each pile and try them in the spaces below.

noun	adjective	noun
	as	as

nouns	adjectives	nouns
gorillas	orange	giraffes
cows	enormous	computers
bananas	wriggly	balloons
Martians	noisy	lemons
trees	clever	raspberries
spaghetti	bouncy	bulldogs

✤ Think of some nouns and adjectives of your own and then cut them out.

Agreeable verbs

What's wrong with this sentence?

The cakes is too hot to eat.

There are too many cakes for the verb 'is'!

The cakes are too hot to eat.

♣ Underline the verb that is wrong in each sentence.

♣ Rewrite the sentences using the correct form of the verb.

My cat have fleas. _____

The children likes playtime. _____

Wesley and Joe is singing. _____

Monster Mo wear huge boots. _____

The main road go past my house. _____

He ask too many questions. _____

Direct and indirect speech

Direct and indirect

This is an example of **direct speech**: 'Hurry up, Liz,' said Harry.
Here is the same statement in **indirect speech**: Harry told Liz to hurry up.

❧ Look at the examples below.

❧ Link each piece of direct speech with the matching indirect speech.

'I'm fed up with this homework,' said Maxine.	Bill ordered Ryan to get his bike.
Karim thought it wasn't fair to blame the dog.	Maxine grumbled about her homework.
'Get your bike!' said Bill to Ryan.	'It's not fair to blame the dog,' said Karim.

❧ Rewrite this in *indirect* speech.

'It's the school trip today,' said Maxine.

'I don't want to go,' said Karim.

'Why not?' asked Bill.

'Because I've forgotton my lunch,' said Karim.

'Don't worry,' said Maxine. 'We'll give you some of ours.'

What's the big idea?

The sentence below has a **main clause** and a **subordinate clause**.

The boy I saw yesterday has a pony.

Main clause:
The boy has a pony.

Subordinate clause:
I saw yesterday.

'The boy has a pony' is the main thing that you are being told. It's the **big idea**.

'I saw yesterday' tells you something less important about the boy. It's the **smaller idea**.

✤ Now look at these:

The chocolate that you gave me was very good.
The pig that can do tricks is in a film.
The clock that doesn't go is on the shelf.
The fish I bought on Saturday is striped.

✤ Write each main clause here:

✤ Make up some more sentences of your own like the ones above.

✤ Continue on the back of this sheet, if you wish.

Joining clauses

Name _____

Put them together

❖ Join each main clause with one subordinate clause to make a complete sentence.

Main clause

I was really surprised

Charlie flew up in the air

Grandad had a shock

Jane wants to be an astronaut

The monkey threw a banana

Subordinate clause

when she grows up.

when he tripped over my skates.

when Ben looked at him.

when he jumped on a trampoline.

when Mum gave me a camera.

❖ Make up two sentences of your own:

	when

	when

Tall, taller, tallest

✤ Fill in the table.

loud	louder	loudest
	smaller	
		highest
old		
		darkest
	lower	
new		
		wildest
	longer	
smooth		

tall   taller   tallest

✤ Now can you draw:

a long snake;	a longer snake?

Comparative adjectives

Name _____

Messy, messier, messiest

messy   messier

messiest

✤ Draw a picture of the wettest day of the year.

✤ Fill in the table.

red	redder	reddest
	hungrier	
		wettest
	finer	
sad		
	bigger	
jolly		
	smellier	
tame		
shiny		

✤ On the back of this sheet write about the messiest bedroom in the world.

Good, better, best

Some words make unusual changes.

many   *more*   *most*

'This programme is boring.'
'This game is even more boring.'
'This book is the most boring of all.'

♣ Finish the table. Think carefully about each word you fill in!

good		best
bad	worse	
		most exciting
	more scared	
	further	

What's the worst programme on TV?

_____

What do your friends think?

_____

What's the most exciting thing you've ever done?

_____

What's the furthest you've been from home?

_____

Comparative adjectives

Bigger and better poems

The Flower

My petals are cooler than water
My stem is smoother than satin
My leaves are greener than emeralds
My scent is sweeter than honey

✤ Use this poem to write about other things, try:
a snowman, a cat or a tree.

A cat

My _____ than _____

My _____ than _____

My _____ than _____

My _____ than _____

A snowman

My _____ than _____

My _____ than _____

My _____ than _____

My _____ than _____

A tree

My _____ than _____

My _____ than _____

My _____ than _____

My _____ than _____

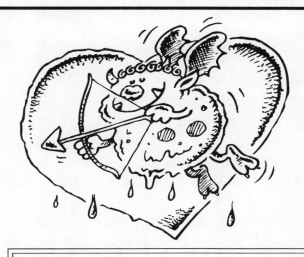

You're the most

✤ Read the poem below.

You're the most
You are like –
the juiciest jelly
the thickest milk shake
the fastest skateboard
the baggiest T-shirt
the brightest socks.

✤ Finish this poem.

A monster's valentine
You are like –
the slimiest slug
the spottiest toad

_____

_____

_____

✤ Now write a 'You're the most' poem of your own.

Capital letters

Name it

Use **capital letters** –
for names of people:
Charlie   **M**elissa   **S**usan   **I**mran

for names of places:
Scotland   **I**taly   **D**ublin   **M**anchester

✤ Fill in the place-names on this road map.
Remember to put in the capital letters!

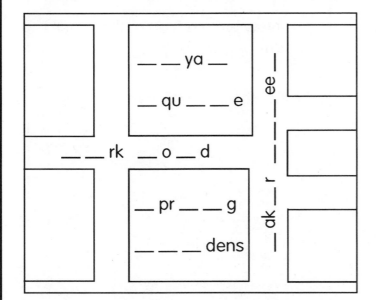

- royal square
- spring gardens
- baker street
- park road

✤ Look at the names
below. Write them on
the register. Put in the
capital letters. Add your
own name, and mark
where it would go.

- joshua carr
- andrew bennett
- karen mills
- jane williams
- carl rogers
- mandy newton

Register

_ _ dr _ _ _ _ _ nn _ _ t

_ _ _ _ h _ a _ _ rr

_ _ r _ n _ _ _ ls

_ _ _ d _ _ _ _ t _ n

_ _ r _ _ _ g _ r _

_____

Capital letters and full stops

Jellysocks

❖ Read the story aloud twice.

❖ Use a pencil to put in full stops and capital letters.

❖ Check by reading it aloud again.

once upon a time there were three frogs one morning they made some pond weed pudding for breakfast it was very hot so they went for a hop on the river bank until their breakfast was cool while they were away a little water beetle called jellysocks came into their house jellysocks ate all the pond weed pudding he turned green and floated away down the river

Commas

Take a break!

Commas are used to show when to pause.

In my pencil-case there are six pencils, an ink pen, some crayons, a pencil-sharpener, two erasers, three paper-clips, an old crisp and a note from my friend.

✤ Add the commas to this list.

In my bag I have six books three folders four stale crusts seven chocolate bar wrappers a plastic frog six football stickers and lots of scrap paper.

✤ Write a list of the things in your pencil-case, bag or pocket. If you can't find anything interesting you can make it up!

Name _____

Time to pause

Commas show you where to pause.

✤ Try to read this story without stopping.

Once upon a time there was a boy called Jack who lived with his mother who worked very hard but still she was very poor even though they had a large brown cow.

✤ Now read this.

Once upon a time there was a princess named Mary, who lived in a palace with her father, the King, who did not like to work, even though he had a lot of land to look after.

✤ Put some commas in the first story.

✤ Write a story for a friend to read aloud. Remember to put in the commas. (You can use the other side of the paper if you wish.)

Sophie and Jake find lost treasure.

What's the question?

✤ Finish this pattern ? ? ?

✤ Read the words. Colour in the **question marks**. Answer the **questions**.

What is your name ? _____

How old are you ? _____

What is your favourite food ? _____

Write about it in the box provided.

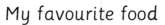

My favourite food

Riddle muddle

A riddle is a kind of question.
Some riddles, and their answers, are
given below, but they are all mixed up!

❖ Cut out the cards.
❖ Put a question mark at the end of each riddle.
❖ Then match the answers to the riddles.

✂ -

A mushroom	How can you make varnish disappear
Where does afternoon come before morning	A shoe
Take the 'r' out of it.	How many sides does a house have
What always travels on foot	In the dictionary
What room has no walls and no door	Two – the inside and the outside

❖ Find or make up some more riddles of your own.

❖ Write them on a separate sheet of paper.

❖ Ask a friend to solve them.

Guess the questions

Adam and Sara went to interview Zelma Bizarre the famous fortune teller. Zelma can see into the future, so she gave the answers before they asked the questions!

✤ Write the questions that Adam and Sara wanted to ask. Don't forget the question marks!

1
In a small town by the sea.
2
I always wash them on Thursdays.
3
I found them under a rock in the desert.
4
Fifty times around the garden every morning.
5
Six cats and four hamsters.
6
I've never done that in my life.

Asking questions

❖ Make each of these **statements** into a **question**.
Remember the question marks.

❖ Now try these.
Write the missing questions.

Example: **Statement:** This is a watch.
           Question: Is this a watch?

Example: **Question:** Did you go to the pictures?
           Statement: Yes, I went to the pictures.

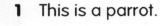

1 This is a parrot.

_____

2 You are a good writer.

_____

3 Jake can fry eggs.

_____

4 The cow can jump over the moon.

_____

5 The bird can sing sweetly.

_____

1 _____

Yes, I had chips for tea.

2 _____

Yes, I went to school.

3 _____

Yes, I saw the show.

4 _____

No, I didn't go out.

5 _____

Yes, I can use question marks.

Exclamation marks

Halt! Danger! Help!

Exclamation marks show that people are speaking loudly! They could be surprised, excited or scared.

Exclamation marks are used in warnings and commands.

✤ Draw pictures to match the labels.

✤ Colour the exclamation marks.

Help! The monster's coming!

Don't go in there!

Look out!

Stop the robber!

✤ Make up some patterns using exclamation marks.

Shock horror game!

✤ Write or draw in some more dangers for this game. (The first one has been done for you.) Use exclamation marks to warn of the danger.

✤ Make up rules and play the game.

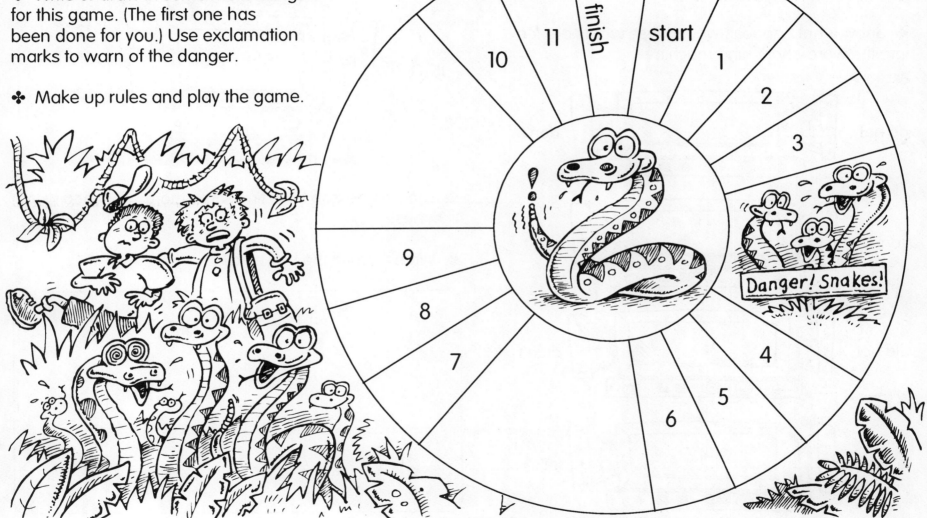

Contractions

Name _____

The word-shortening machine

❖ This machine is sometimes able to shorten words.

❖ Show what happens when these words are fed into the word-shortening machine.

is not   is → not   isn't

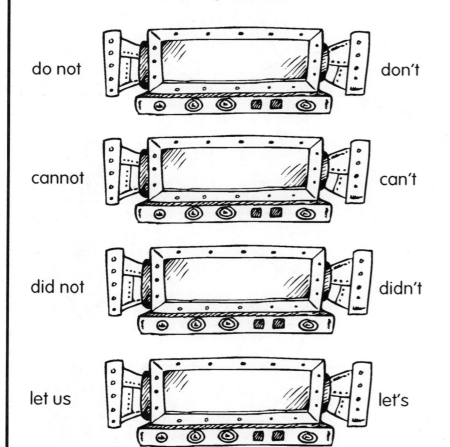

do not   don't

cannot   can't

did not   didn't

let us   let's

❖ Look in books to try to find some more shortened words like these.

❖ Write them in the box below.

Teacher Timesavers: Grammar

Whose pet?

's = belongs to

The buffalo belongs to Beth.

It is **Beth's buffalo**.

♣ Label the pictures.
Some have been done for you.

Beth has a buffalo.
Zoe has a zebra.
Wally has a walrus.
The dog belongs to Debra.
Benny has a beetle.
Shirley has a shark.
Chris has a crocodile.
The mouse belongs to Mark.

Beth's buffalo		Wally's walrus	

			Mark's mouse

Possessive apostrophes

Spot the apostrophes

Can you spot the difference?

The pirate's treasure

The pirates' treasure

The **apostrophe** is at the end here because there is more than one pirate.

✤ Put in the apostrophes.

The monkeys tail

The dogs bone

The girls pencils

✤ Look at these unusual ones.

The children's chocolate
The fairy's wands
The fairies' wands

The monkeys tails

The dogs bone

The girls pencils

✤ Now put the apostrophes in these.

The babys nappies
The babies nappies
The ladys shoe
The ladies shoe

Gina's gerbil

❖ Put the apostrophes in the story below.
Remember: 's = belongs to.

There were a lot of pets in Ginas house. She had a cat, a rabbit, a gerbil, six hamsters and two budgies.

One day Ginas gerbil was missing. Gina looked in the rabbits hutch, the cats basket and the hamsters cage. She knew he would not be in the budgies cage because it was too high up.

She went to watch childrens television. Then she heard a loud noise in the kitchen. What a mess! There was the gerbil, eating the crisps in Ginas lunch-box. He had knocked over the babys milk and made a mess of mums bag.

❖ Draw a picture to go with the story.

Speech marks

Name _____

Who's talking?

'   ' **Speech marks** show that someone is talking.

'Are you coming out to play?' said Binky.
'No, I'm watching TV,' said Dinky.

❦ Write out the conversations. Put in the speech marks, and any other punctuation.

'_____,' said Powerful Pete. '_____,' said Strong Steve.

_____

_____

_____

Name _____

Reasons to write

Why do we write?   ♣ Jot down your ideas here.

♣ Keep a record of the writing you do and see today.
Continue on the back of this sheet if you wish.

Writing I have done

Writing I have seen

Exploring picture writing

Secret messages

This message was left at the entrance to a cave.

| I | have gone that way | for four days | a long way | then I'm coming back |

✤ Draw these messages.

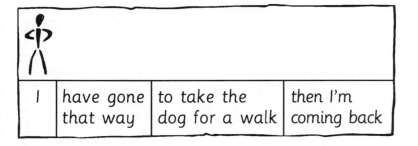

| I | have gone that way | to take the dog for a walk | then I'm coming back |

| I | have gone that way | to meet my friend | and buy a bottle of milk | then I'm coming back |

✤ Finish these messages.

| I | have gone that way | | then I'm coming back |

| I | have gone that way | | then I'm coming back |

✤ Now make up some messages of your own.

✤ Draw them on the back of this sheet.

Word origins

Etymology

etymon = the meaning of a word
-ology = the study of
etymology = the study of word meanings

graffiti – Italian for *scribbling*

chocolate – Aztec for *bitter water*

calculator – from the Latin for *pebble*. Pebbles were used for counting.

✤ Find the origins of these words:

telephone _____

television _____

computer _____

technology _____

video _____

biscuit _____

Foreign exchange

The world's most common languages are:

English *Hello*   Chinese *Ni hao*   Spanish *Hola*

English uses many words from other languages.

Examples: algebra – Arabic
safari – Swahili (Africa)
llama – Spanish
khaki – Urdu

✤ Find the origin of these words:

guitar _____   dentist _____

pyjamas _____   anorak _____

banana _____   pasta _____

camouflage _____   yoghurt _____

✤ Write a story using at least six of these words.
Use the back of this sheet.

Top ten words

Some words are used more often than others.

These are the 'Top Ten' words:

1	the
2	of
3	and
4	a
5	to
6	in
7	is
8	you
9	that
10	it

✤ Read this passage. Circle any 'top ten' words.

A rabbit has long ears and soft fur. It lives in a hutch made out of wood. You can keep rabbits outside, if it is not freezing. In the winter you should move them to a place that is not too cold.

✤ On the back of this sheet write a few sentences about a different animal. See how many of the 'top ten' words you use and write them in the box below.

Using a thesaurus

Name _____

Treasure chest

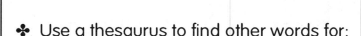

Thesaurus comes from the Greek word for 'treasure'.

A thesaurus is a treasure chest of words.

✤ Read the story.

✤ Use a thesaurus to find words to replace the words in bold type.

Example: **shower** could be changed to downpour or cloudburst.

Tariq was caught in a **shower** _____.

His **coat** _____ got very **wet** _____.

'I don't want to **arrive** _____ at my new

office like this,' he thought. 'I must go to a shop

and **choose** _____ a new coat. It's a pity

I don't **own** _____ a **car** _____.

✤ Use a thesaurus to find other words for:

old _____

_____

dry _____

_____

food _____

_____

sleep _____

_____

Nice words

Here are some words for **nice**.
Can you find more in the thesaurus?

pleasant delightful agreeable enjoyable good lovely

✤ Choose a different word to replace **nice** each time it appears in the story below.

Saturday was a **nice** _____ day. We went to town to do

some shopping. The weather was **nice** _____. We had

some **nice** _____ ice-cream and a **nice** _____

walk round the shopping centre. I bought a **nice** _____

new scarf. Then we went home.

✤ Write about something you really enjoyed on the back of this sheet. Use as many different words as you can for **nice**.

Types of writing

Name _____

Favourite stories

What kind of stories do you like?

 Adventure

 Romance

 Ghost

 Funny

 Animal

 Mystery

♣ Write about your favourite story. Title: _____

My favourite bit of the story was...
The characters are...

♣ Jot down some ideas for a story of your own.

How will your story begin?
Characters

Name _____

Fact and fiction

FACT

Fab Facts About Football

by J. Smith

The first FA cup final to take place at Wembley was Bolton vs West Ham in 1923.

FICTION

WANDA of the WANDERERS

by M. Ball

Wanda dribbled the ball towards the goal area. This was her big chance!

Both these books are about football. One is **fact** and one is **fiction**.

✤ Draw covers for two books about the same subject. One book should be fact and one fiction.

✤ Write or draw a page from each book.

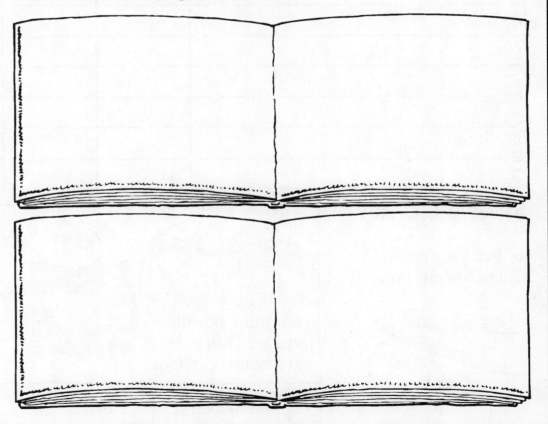

Types of writing

Name _____

Finding your way around books

❖ Choose eight books from the bookshelf – four story books and four information books.   ❖ Find and tick.

Name of book	Title page	Author	Illustrator	Publisher	Contents	Index

❖ Look at these pages.

❖ Tick the boxes.
Colour the pictures.

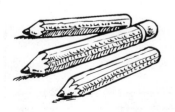

The giant panda lives in China. It eats bamboo shoots.

'Come on, Ann,' shouted Peter. 'Let's run away!'

☐ Information   ☐ Story   ☐ Information   ☐ Story

Modern fairy tale

♣ Write a modern fairy tale.

Use these words in your story:

| computer | telephone |
| popstar | video |

♣ Write the name for your main character in the spaces below.

One day _____ was drinking a can of lemonade. _____

shook the can and – WHOOSH! A genie appeared from the can...

What does it mean?

❖ Match the playground language to the right sentences.

Over here, mate

Get out of my way

Gerroff

Give us a crisp, Gaz

That's ours – give it here

Hey, give us the ball

May I have a crisp please, Gary?

Will you pass the ball, please?

Please come over here, my friend.

I believe that's ours – may we have it, please?

Would you mind getting off my foot, please.

Excuse me, please.

Language map

♣ Look at this 'language map' of a school dinner hall.

I don't like custard on beans!

Stay in the line!

Put your trays here.

Don't sit on the packed lunch table!

I've got yoghurt on my nose.

Sit down Charlotte!

Can I go out now please?

♣ Try to listen to the things people say – at home, in school, in the street, at the swimming baths...

♣ Make your own 'language map' of a place you know well in the box below. Give it a title.

Poems to say aloud

❖ Read this poem. Practise and perform it to a friend.

OK gimme
OK gimme
2 quarterpounders
2 cheeseburgers
4 side orders of french fries
2 Coca-Colas
2 Doc Peppers

All to go
Yeh all to go
We've got to go

Over 35 million sold
Over 35 million sold

OK that will be 9 dollars and 50
Have a nice day
Have a nice day.

Martyn Wiley

The poet, Martyn Wiley, heard these words in a café in America. It is often possible to make a poem from the words you hear around you.

❖ Collect words and phrases in assembly, in PE, in the dinner hall.

❖ Note them down on this sheet, then make them into a poem to say aloud.

Collected words and phrases.

(NB Source of poem, Video: *Count to five and say I'm alive* Team Video production, CANALOT, 222 Kensal Road, London W10 5BN)

Teacher Timesavers: Grammar

Banana split

Kim has asked her friend Dina how to make banana splits.

Dina:
'Well, you get a banana and cut it – you cut it the long way and you have to have a long dish to put it in. Then you put scoops of ice-cream between the two bits of banana – and then you can put cherries on top and pour on cream or chocolate sauce.

Kim:
'I can't remember all that. Will you write out the recipe for me?'

♣ Write out the recipe for banana split.

Remember that you just need to write out the important facts.

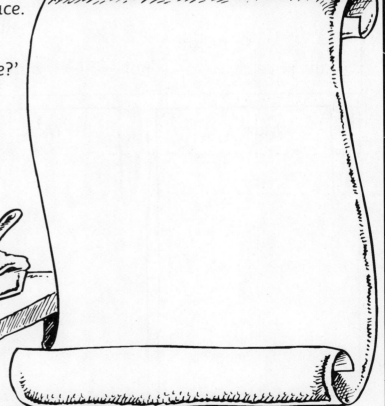

From written to spoken language

What would you like?

♣ Choose two things for Max and two things for Mary.

What will Max and Mary say to the waitress?

Words to help you

I	beans	toast	please
like	would	burger	chips
fruit juice		hot dog	milk shake

Max:

Mary:

Opposites

Words of **opposite** meaning are called **antonyms**.

❖ Join these antonyms in matching pairs. The first one is done for you.

crooked	shrink
cold	valley
bright	straight
grow	warm
mountain	dull

freezing	seldom
often	remember
private	smooth
forget	boiling
rough	public

❖ Read the story, then find antonyms for the words in bold type.

Mystic Malcolm was the **best** _____ magician in the world. His

tricks never went **wrong** _____. He could make a rabbit **appear**

_____ and do **clever** _____ things with cards. One night

he made the whole audience disappear. 'No magician is **better**

_____ than I am,' said Malcolm. 'The world will **remember**

_____ me forever!'

Name _____

Sounds like...

Here are some words that sound alike.   ✤ Draw the right picture for each thing and cross out the wrong word.

a fruit	an animal	a tree	to lock things with
pear pair	hair hare	beach beech	quay key

a plant	animal feet	a bucket	an animal
flower flour	pause paws	pail pale	bare bear

Do you know the meaning of all the words crossed out?   ✤ Check them in a dictionary if you're not sure.

Teacher Timesavers: Grammar

Different words – same meaning

Synonyms are words which have almost the same meaning.

♣ Match the synonyms. Two have been done to start you off.

donkey	bun
bowl	wizard
dirt	ass
big	dish
cake	soil
magician	large

drink	thin
sorrow	ban
middle	under
paradise	beverage
beneath	sleek
prohibit	puzzle
quiet	heaven
riddle	sadness
slender	silent
smooth	centre

✤ Read the story.
Find synonyms for the words in bold type.

Aysha lost her cat, Lucy. She **ran** _____ to her friend's

house _____. Aysha's friend was **called** _____

Hannah. 'Please help me to **search** _____ for Lucy,'

begged _____ Aysha. 'All right,' **said** _____ Hannah.

'We'll **start** _____ near your house.' 'Wait,' said Aysha.

'There's Lucy. She's going into your **outhouse** _____.'

Synonyms and antonyms

Same and different

❖ Draw lines to join the words that mean the same.

young	sour
bitter	highest
top	fluid
same	brief
liquid	immature
short	equal

❖ Draw lines to join the words with opposite meaning.

hard	big
yes	cold
slim	no
happy	soft
little	plump
hot	sad

❖ Find antonyms for these words.

young
bitter
top
same
liquid
short

❖ Find synonyms for these words.

hard
yes
slim
happy
little
hot

❖ Fill this chart. Extend it on the back of this sheet if you wish.

word	synonym	antonym
tiny	little	big
high		
wet		
glad		
ill		
love		
yell		

Place-names

♣ Draw a picture for each of these place-names.

Mullingar = crooked mill	Pomfret = broken bridge	Shugborough = hill haunted by goblins

What do you think these places look like?   Frogwell   Appletreewick   Sevenoaks

♣ Draw a picture for each one on the back of this sheet.

Name that place!

---

wick or **wich** = dwelling place

Example:
Cheswick = a place where cheese was made.

What does **Butterwick** mean?

_____

---

caster, chester = castle

Find three place-names which contain **caster**
or **chester**.

_____

_____

---

beck, burn = stream

♣ What do these place-names mean?

Blackburn = _____

Troutbeck = _____

♣ Prepare and practise a chant of place-name sounds. You can set it to percussion if you wish.

Example: Say these place-names aloud.

♣ Find out what **bally** means.

'Ballymoney
Ballycastle
Ballymena
Ballyclare'

Monster bargains

✤ Draw or write about more bargains for monsters.

Try to make them sound really special.

Persuasive language

Astronaut specials

♣ Draw and write about more astronaut specials.

Make sure they sound like things an astronaut would really need.

The puppet show

♣ Make a poster for a puppet show in your class.

♣ Remember to put the day, the time and where it will happen.

♣ Make your poster look as interesting as possible.

puppet show

On: _____

At: _____

In: _____

Persuasive language

Name _____

The amazing snowball machine

You have invented a wonderful machine for making snowballs.

✤ Write and draw an advertisement for your machine.
It should be exciting so that everyone will want to buy it.

✤ Use the back of this sheet for an advertisement for something else you have invented.

Notes and letters: 1

♣ Write a letter to the Speedy Bike Shop to order a new bike.

♣ Write a note inviting a friend to come to tea.

Notes and letters: 2

❖ Write a note to your teacher. Ask for a day off. Say why you want it.

❖ Write a secret note to a friend.

60 Storm Street.

Dear Mr Carr
Ryan was off school yesterday because he fell over the dog and landed on his gran.

Mrs Bell

come to my den tonight. L

DOG

Which way?

Naima has just started a new school and wants to know the way to the post office.

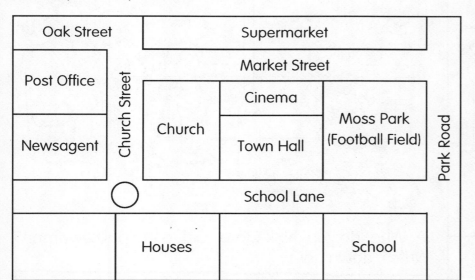

Oak Street	Supermarket			
Post Office	Market Street			
Newsagent	Church	Cinema	Moss Park (Football Field)	
		Town Hall		
	School Lane			
	Houses		School	

Church Street

Park Road

You go down here and round where we play football then you go near where my mum works...

❖ Read the directions Sarah gave her.

❖ Can you give better directions?

Language study

Writing for an audience

Telling the story

✤ Read this first.

✤ What do you think Clare said to the policewoman? Write it down here.

Police report

✤ Look carefully at this picture.

✤ Finish the police report describing what happened. Continue on the back of this sheet if you have to.

Remember that police reports just describe the facts.

Date: 4th October   Time: 4pm

I was called to the scene of an accident on

Beech Lane at 1.30pm. Mark Brown, aged 10yrs

6mths, of 2 Beech Lane had...

Nouns

Name _____

Name the object!

A **noun** is a word used as the name of a person, place or thing.

✤ Fill in the labels with the nouns which 'name' the pictures below.

Test your memory

♣ Look at the picture for two minutes. Then cover it.

♣ Write down all the things you remember.

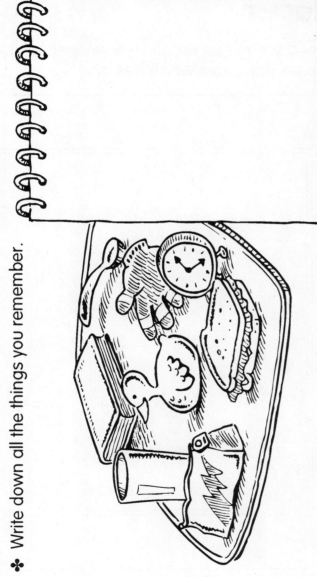

♣ Write a short story about three of the objects on the tray.

Name _____

Adjectives

Describing places

An **adjective** is a word used to describe something.

❧ Draw a scene that is definitely *not* peaceful. Write some adjectives which describe it.

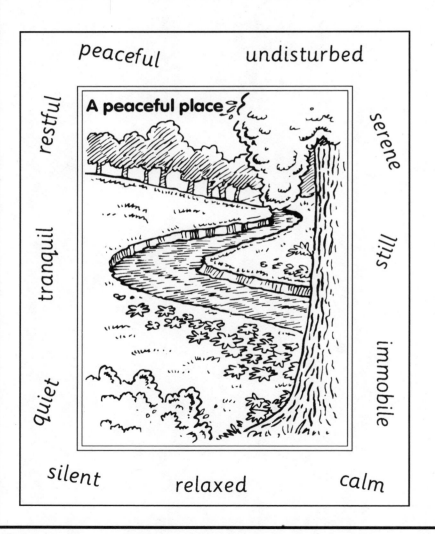

peaceful   undisturbed

restful

A peaceful place

serene

tranquil

still

quiet

immobile

silent   relaxed   calm

Teacher Timesavers: Grammar

Name _____

Describing things

This racing car is surrounded by adjectives which mean fast.

♣ Draw and describe a snail. Use a thesaurus to find words for 'slow'.

Adjectives

Describing a person

✤ Draw a picture of someone you know.

✤ Write words and phrases which describe the person in the frame. You can use a thesaurus.

whopping
titanic
immense
gargantuan   huge
monstrous
mountainous
enormous

Name _____

Describing a character

♣ This is a picture of Super Sal. Use a thesaurus to find more words to describe her.

♣ Draw and describe another character called Hopeless Harriet.

brave   fierce   bold

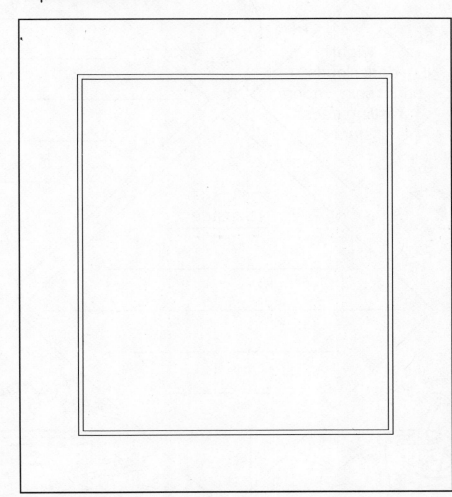

Teacher Timesavers: Grammar

Nouns and adjectives

Name _____

Diamond poems

❖ Read this poem.

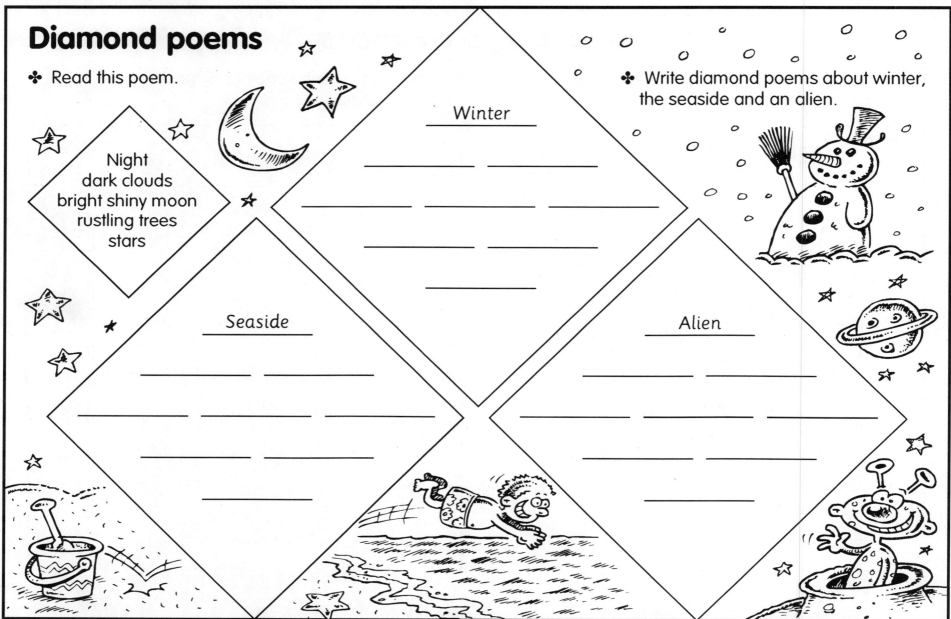

Night
dark clouds
bright shiny moon
rustling trees
stars

Winter
_____ _____
_____
_____ _____

❖ Write diamond poems about winter, the seaside and an alien.

Seaside
_____ _____
_____
_____

Alien
_____ _____
_____
_____

Same sound list poems

In the supermarket I saw

1 bent banana
2 green grapes
3 oval oranges
4 pink peas
and
5 cool carrots

♣ Finish these poems.

In the supermarket I saw

1 pot of polish

2 jars of jam

3 _____

4 _____

and

5 _____

In the safari park I saw

1 _____

2 _____

3 _____

4 _____

and

5 _____

In the _____ I saw

1 _____

2 _____

3 _____

4 _____

and

5 _____

Nouns

Word inventions

✤ Cut up the nouns.

✤ Put them together in different pairs, such as:

| car | phone | | library | book |

✤ Think about what a **cake tree** or a **dog hat** might look like.

✤ Try drawing some of the new objects you have invented. Use the back of this sheet if you wish.

radio	book	car	phone
pool	computer	house	school
library	hat	dog	cake
jelly	lamp	bridge	bag
dream	key	tree	camera

Name _____

What are they doing?

A **verb** is a word which tells us what we do.

✤ Read the words opposite.

✤ Write each one under the picture that it matches.

run	drink
wave	talk
hop	sit
jump	fall
crawl	laugh

Verbs

Name _____

Message in a bottle

Do you know what verbs are?

✤ Circle all the verbs in this message.

> 'I am on a desert island. My ship has sunk.
>
> 'Please rescue me.'

Verbs are very useful things. Without them you would not be able to tell people what has happened and you would not be able to ask them to do something.

Imagine

You are on a boat trip deep in the rain forest. Your canoe has turned over and you have been washed up on the river bank.

Write a message to put in a bottle. Say what has happened and ask for help.

Circle all the verbs you use in the message.

In the future

We use the **future tense** of verbs to talk about what we are going to do or what will happen in the future.

♣ Read the speech bubbles. Underline the future tense verbs. The first one has been done for you.

♣ Write about what *you* would like to do in the future.

Verbs: past tense

What did you do?

We use the **past tense** to tell about what we have done.

♣ Write a story about something you did a long time ago.

In my day, we didn't have computers to play with. We played with marbles and listened to the wireless.

BLEEP!

♣ Look back at the verbs you used. Underline the ones that are in the past tense.

Yesterday, today and tomorrow

♣ Complete this table.

Yesterday	Today	Tomorrow
(walk) I walked	I walk	I shall walk
(play) she _____	she _____	she _____
(write) they _____	they _____	they _____
(swam) we _____	we _____	we _____
(eat) you _____	you _____	you _____
(count) I _____	I _____	I _____
(sing) they _____	they _____	they _____
(draw) he _____	he _____	he _____

Verbs: future tense

Name _____

Time machine in the future

You looked into a time machine and could see 50 years into the future.

❧ Write to tell your friend about it.

In the future there will be...

Time machine in the past

You looked into your time machine to see what life was like in prehistoric times when people lived in caves.

✤ Write to tell your friends about it.

In prehistoric times people used to...

Name _____

Adverbs

How is it done?

Adverbs tell you *how* something is done.

The baby cried.   The baby cried **loudly**.

✤ Put each of these adverbs in the right sentence.   *carefully   loudly   quickly   dangerously*

Ali did not pour the milk

The children ran

Ann balanced on the cliff

The teacher shouted

_____   _____   _____   _____

✤ Draw a picture and write a matching sentence for each of these adverbs. Use the back of this sheet.

slowly   angrily   greedily

Underlining adverbs

The underlined words in this story are adverbs.

When the monster rose up <u>angrily</u> from the canal we were <u>very</u> scared. We ran <u>quickly</u> to the police station and all started shouting <u>excitedly</u>.

❖ Continue the story above and on the back of this sheet if you wish.

❖ Underline the adverbs you have used.

❖ Draw a picture of your story on the back of this sheet.

Adverbs

Adverbs from adjectives

You can make adverbs from **adjectives**:

The girl spoke in a *quiet* voice.
The girl spoke *quietly*.

♣ Try this one:
The baby gave a *happy* smile.

The baby smiled _____

♣ Make adverbs from these adjectives, then make up a sentence using each adverb you have listed.

loud _____   horrible _____

clear _____   merry _____

♣ Write spelling rules for changing these adjectives to adverbs. The first one is done for you.

careful – *carefully*
You add 'ly'. No need to change any letters.

useful

terrible

happy

greedy

Word quilt

♣ Colour the verbs red.
Colour the nouns yellow.
Colour the adjectives green.
Colour the adverbs blue.

♣ Write a sentence in the pillow using at least one noun, one verb, one adjective and one adverb from the quilt.

sadly	lazy	aeroplane	eat
jump	shoe	quickly	little
cat	angrily	funny	sing
happy	loudly	run	apple

Prepositions

Name _____

Where is it?

Prepositions tell us where things are.

✤ Look at these sentences.

✤ Write the preposition here

The dog is under the table.

_____ under _____

The girl is on the moon.

_____

The cat is up the tree.

_____

The fox jumped over the gate.

_____

✤ Write three more sentences for: inside   outside   behind ————

Read and draw

❖ Read these short descriptions, then draw a picture for each one.

The big dog was sitting near the armchair with his bone. There was a bowl of water on the floor between the dog and the bone.

There was an old cottage among the trees. It had roses around the door. Beneath the front window was a bench to sit on.

Prepositions

Where does it go?

❖ Look at the instructions. Then draw each thing in the right place.

Put the cat on the sofa.

Put the photo on the shelf.

Put the radio behind the photo.

Put the cup on the television.

Put the duck next to the cup.

Put the telephone under the table.

Put it where?

✤ Read the instructions, then draw these things in the right place.

Put the elephant in the deck-chair.

Put the sun-glasses on the elephant.

Put the sun-hat under the table.

Put the sausage in the sun-hat.

Put the jelly on top of the sausage.

Put the ice-cream at the end of the elephant's trunk.

Prepositions

The untidy room game: 1

✤ Play this game with a partner.
He or she will need: **The untidy room game: 2**.

✤ Do not show each other your sheets.

You have lost these things.

✤ Ask your partner to find them on her/his sheet and describe where they are.

✤ Draw them on your sheet.

✤ Then check with your partner's sheet. How many did you get right?

The untidy room game: 2

❖ Play this game with a partner.
He or she will need: **The untidy room game: 1**.

❖ Do not show each other your sheets.

You have lost these things.

❖ Ask your partner to find them on her/his sheet and describe where they are.

❖ Draw them on your sheet.

❖ Then check with your partner's sheet. How many did you get right?

Pronouns

Who did what?

A **pronoun** is a word which replaces a noun, such as:

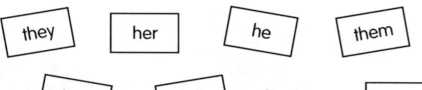

they   her   he   them

him   us   she   it

✤ Look at the pronouns above.

✤ Use them to replace the <u>underlined words</u>.

The robber stole jewels and hid <u>the jewels</u> under his bed.

The next day <u>the robber</u> looked for <u>the jewels</u>.

'<u>The jewels</u> have gone!' <u>the robber</u> cried.

'Do you mean that bag of junk?' said his mother.

'I gave <u>the bag</u> to the police jumble sale.'

'Oh no!' said the robber.

So <u>his mother</u> told <u>the robber</u> she was sorry.

140

Name _____

Pronouns:

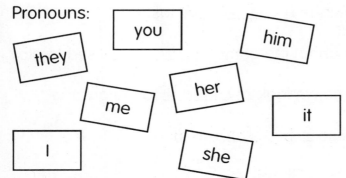

they   you   him   her   me   it   I   she

❖ Read this nonsense rhyme.

❖ Circle the pronouns.

They told me you had been to her,

And mentioned me to him:

She gave me a good character,

But said I could not swim.

Lewis Carroll

He, she, it

❖ Read the story below.

❖ Replace all the underlined nouns with pronouns.

Rosy went to town. Sam bought <u>Rosy</u> _____ a cake. Rosy gave

<u>the cake</u> _____ to Dan. <u>Dan</u> _____ invited Rosy and Sam

to tea. <u>Dan and Rosy and Sam</u> _____ ate the cake together.

Pronouns

Name _____

Fill the gaps

Pronouns:

| it | | I |

| he | | you |

| we | |

| she | | they |

❖ Put the right pronoun in each space.

Example: Our puppy is naughty. <u>He</u> ate my shoes.

I like my new bike because _____ is fast.

My grandma told us about the games _____ used to play.

The car broke down so we took _____ to the garage.

I like hamsters because _____ are funny.

Don't fall or _____ will hurt yourself.

I called for Jenny and _____ went to play in her garden.

Teacher Timesavers: Grammar

What's 'it'?

❖ Read this poem called 'What's it?'

Yesterday I made it,
today I wasted it.
My brother beat it,
but I couldn't stand the noise.

Tomorrow I'll keep it,
the other day I lost it,
killing it in the playground,
talking to the boys.

Ian McMillan

Can you guess what it is?

❖ Write some 'What's it?' riddles of your own. Then challenge your friends to guess what 'it' is.

Example: It has four legs, a head and a foot. What is it?

Answer: A bed.

Conjunctions

Make a connection

Conjunctions join words, clauses and sentences.

and   but   because

Example: I ate my supper. I went to bed.
            I ate my supper and I went to bed.

❖ Choose the best word to join each of these.

❖ Write out the new sentences.

I wanted to go out. My Gran wouldn't let me. _____

Mike can't come to school. He is ill. _____

I've done my homework. I've put my books away. _____

Gemma can't ride her bike. The brakes don't work. _____

Amir's dog ran away. It soon came back. _____

Look out for these conjunctions!

then   *since*   though
      or   *if*
however   so   unless